T0267405

BLOOD

BLOOD

TYLER PENNOCK

BRICK BOOKS

Library and Archives Canada Cataloguing in Publication
Title: Blood / Tyler Pennock.
Names: Pennock, Tyler, 1977– author.
Identifiers: Canadiana (print) 20220250596 | Canadiana (ebook) 20220250618 |
ISBN 9781771315814 (softcover) | ISBN 9781771315821 (HTML) |
ISBN 9781771315838 (PDF)
Subjects: LCGFT: Poetry.
Classification: LCC PS8631.E56 B56 2022 | DDC C811/.6—dc23

Copyright © Tyler Pennock, 2022

We gratefully acknowledge the Canada Council for the Arts, the Government of
Canada through the Canada Book Fund, and the Ontario Arts Council for their support
of our publishing program.

Edited by Joshua Whitehead.
Cover by Ovila Mailhot.
Author photo by Michael White.
The book is set in Dante.
Design by Marijke Friesen.
Printed and bound by Coach House Printing.

Brick Books
487 King St. W.
Kingston, ON
K7L 2X7
www.brickbooks.ca

Though much of the work of Brick Books takes place on the ancestral lands of the
Anishinaabeg, Haudenosaunee, Huron-Wendat, and Mississaugas of the Credit
peoples, our editors, authors, and readers from many backgrounds are situated from
coast to coast to coast in Canada on the traditional and unceded territories of over six
hundred nations who have cared for Turtle Island from time immemorial. While living
and working on these lands, we are committed to hearing and returning the rightful
imaginative space to the poetries, songs, and stories that have been untold, under-told,
wrongly told, and suppressed through colonization.

Dedicated to Ian W. Clarke

Giwachiyenaanig Gimishoomisinaanag

Before dawn
everything slows

like a held breath
waiting to see what survived
     an embrace
     with change

a meeting
sung in water droplets
     cold leaves
     and branches
     shrinking the air
     around them

Beads
grow like
fruit

supernal

If we think
the air's capacity
     constant

and perception implies existence

mornings are
a cautious awakening
where water speaks of clouds

No one wants to learn who was taken
while we slept

and yet –

there is always birdsong
breaking the quiet

letting us know
it's safe to rise again

•

Morning sounds
reaching westward

well ahead of the sun's first light –

    new growth waiting
    to cover the earth

as water
    rushes through ice fractures
    led by warmth's advance

thawing space enough to peer through

fringes contorting
to occupy the lens
of a new medium

Receding lines cradle the cold
    a distorted retreat from
    warming air

ice exhaling a new land
with nutrient enough
to grow in

but still hesitant
    withholding

jealously guarding
    shapes
    features
    structures

made the night before

   •

I lied
I won't see you tomorrow

I'm not coming home

I know –

like a light breath
there's no voice to make my effort real

I hope you won't mind
my quietness in this –

instead of naming the connections
or even trying

I'd rather leave
     lights trailing away
     teasing out a long highway
     from me to you

  •

Imagine me searching
instead of leaving

the way fog searches for light
        wanting to be pierced

how light waits for clouds
        wanting to be softened
        blurred in return

how torn skin
waits for the warm flood

where each thrust softens the blade's edge a little

A compromise –

        formed from mutual harm
        you can't bear to see the end of

Growth is a maddening act
and ghosts are eager to run free

        •

This is gonna hurt

After we met, I had the same dream every night for months.

The ice was wet, eager, urgent, and heavy, covering everything in sheets. When it caught and hardened, it pulled like fast pavement on determined flesh. Windows, walls, clothes, light, heat, colour, breath, skin, blood, bone . . . everything seemed to sing its tiredness in gravity, begging to be released from connection.

Except the faces.

Hundreds of people wearing colourless coats passed me as I moved. And they smiled. Fixed smiles, without even a tremble, watched me while they continued past. As I turned to look, those smiles continued facing me. Their bodies couldn't provide any boundary to the glare – the smiles swam through other features.

In others, their necks twisted, limits announced by grinding, snapping sounds.

Like the ice, their faces had a hunger for warm things. These were eyes that knew their next meal, lips that coveted texture; pupils and tongues that owned everything they took in.

I turned to a window, hoping to find in my own face something like safety, comfort.

Ice was already forming on my cheeks, pulling colour – skin – the light in me downward.

Before I turned away, the reflection filled with hundreds of eyes – and mouths, inhaling.

•

If you experience enough pain and fear
you'll learn to ignore its place

let it fill you

How does blood hurt?
How does blood know quiet
when it can't dry and set
around the wound?

– the first lines I wrote

in a notebook I carry

to be remembered

fearing the distance
and time that will pass
through the memories of us – yet

I don't want to scratch the paper
I don't want to repeat

what you did

to let the world in

this time

•

I have so many writing books
given by loving friends –
friends I left
before they could ask
what I wrote

So many blank pages

I feel like I've earned them

the way an ocean can earn fog
        colder than the body beside it

each page wanting to hold something
but never pieces of me

a whiteness so repetitive
that I'm scared to mark it
        scared of what features the ink might contain
        for others to focus on

Being featureless is powerful
especially in memory

without a mark to focus on
at least they're still searching

    •

Should I survive
the spring

it won't be because I'm strong
    few of us are

We're like girdled trees
    hard
    thirsty
    and suffocating

forests gleaming
beautiful briefly
bursting red and brown
in early death

shaped this way
by governing
hegemonizing
dominating hands

whiter
softer

      than bark
      and yet

small aggressions, multiplied
clot and choke

more efficient than
      knives
      axes

There's no blood spray
to outline a darkened killer
no sap rushing out
         to stick
         hold

stop the blades that release it

   •

Today a man tried touching me
claiming to feel
brief rises of skin over surging veins
through air density

      reiki or some shit

searching for unseen parts of me
implying I could notice

over the alarmed
autonomic retreats
my belly made

my awareness
vacillating
between his thirst
and the table he found

vigilant

at the weekend-emptied
construction site

my reactions
my functions stolen
      my hesitations his millinery plumage
      my sensations his courtship
      my awareness his pageantry

Can you feel that?

How about that?

I lied
Anything to end it and get the breakfast I was promised

•

What is it about us
and the beauty they see

amassing around their focus
imagined qualities collecting
accreting their desire

a protostar
        to be marked
        held, kept, had
        surveyed before it evolves again

I wish their desire could give better shape to it
than the feelings I get from their craving

Why do they want it?
Why must they *feel* it?

As if all their imaginings
were oysters and pearls
the gathering centres
        a ripening
to be interrupted

And here I am questioning
the obvious –

they think that because it's beautiful
it doesn't belong to the body it's in

    •

We

We all want

Some *want*
harder than others

adeptly piercing
our resistance
our lack of consent
in a fevered pitch

erecting
dams
bridges
railroads
pipelines

and celebrating their ingenuity

They feel like a sickness
that enters easily
and replicates unseen

until a fever begins
burning through cells

I worry that we've been fevered for too long
and our body doesn't know how to heal anymore

as the constant friction
and force of intent

gives way to calluses
                in flesh too tired to resist

•

Cities are alive
and speaking –

behave, the skyscrapers say
a threat carried in their mastery
                at hiding the sun

a potency
suggested by their height
and abundance
crowding over me

windows like breeding eyes
pointed out and downward
        multiplying antipathy

like teachers
        building power
        through a classroom's silence

their authority
endorsed
encouraged

by every unchallenged abuse
until I'm left like these buildings

static

with hundreds of holes

                      fixed and open

•

Students
children

      experiencing un-countered violence
      will re-create it in others

   •

There's an expression I'd heard
that old people are full of earth –

whole, rich, dark
over time

wounds and recovery
tumbling through a life
a dual orbit shrinking

roots, insects
          digging
          dilating
          tearing
spaces the air can enter

like the dirt
we grow
because of

burrowed holes
that our nature
can escape through

          •

Earth can bend
around us

cradle our feet
as our weight digs in
        give way when needed

I like how the softer
                wetter soils
hang on to you a little longer

Mud rises
        reaching
cresting higher
above your shoe

vacuum-gripped
your steps
        slowed

the dirt holds on
limiting your impact
        the damage
        your weight
induces

until your own ache
sweat and burn
join the effort

to stop you

•

There's an impatience in us
we're running

unable to sit
        in
the space of a moment

It's like putting blinders on a horse
        cupping darkness
        over eyes evolved
        to see the edges

sleeping just to wake
fearing the dream's
prismatic influence
        on our vision

ending beauty
        and joy
because they feel
too much like
anxiety

        •

You've left just a scratch
not even a crack in who I was

      I didn't need more
      than a sliver of light

but my clenching wound
splintered colours inside
me still
           briefly

and now, staring at a new page
on a bus headed east

I wish snow could fall on this
      seal my skin around
      the impact of you
decelerate the light
hold it longer
slow the outward flow

I created when I left you

      But winter is leaving us

•

Bones are the hardest part of us
but have you ever scratched one?

When the skin of a bone fails
    marrow comes forward to knit
    reclaiming what the tissue struggled to hold

      blood's purpose
      its starting place a wound
      its ending a geography remade

•

So many men
mistake
            acquiescence
for desire

            allowance
for an invitation to push again

assume their age is a
barrier
we both agree to traverse
            (an ice-covered slope
            with a discernible base)

that we share the same glaucoma
            (permanent blindness
            to periphery)

Lately
I hardly use conversation –

            when it's for money
            we see the same thing

but

when I'm saturated
with the smell of
sweat-sweetened cologne

I
keep
wondering

where the difference was

hoping there's still a barrier between us

  that it's not lost
  somewhere inside me

 •

Once, the john slipped inside me
accidentally

(we had agreed not to let that happen)

he didn't notice

Accidentally

I couldn't tell which was going to break out first

a radiating fire-throb
        electric singe
        of pain

or room-shrinking
panicked gasping
awareness that

        something was
            wrong

my thoughts
sensing the double incapacity

        outstripped them both

faster than water can escape a breaking glass

    •

You're thinking about it
        aren't you?

Wondering if the water's pain is possible

thinking about
        throwing full glasses on the floor

to try and witness
        what I meant

if there's truth to the line
        or if I'm tricking you

Funny that

how people understand shock
and violence
                        differently

Some of us ride the sensation
nerves barely able to hold it
pain threatening to
                        arc the skin

while others
smash
        glass

repeatedly

        •

I enjoyed the john's unselfishness
the way he openly
described
        planned how
we'd fuck

generous in assurances
of trust
                care
gentleness

meticulously averting
        any possible harm

but

a man who can't consider
pain's probability
won't acknowledge
        harm's impact

until he's finished

        •

Not that I would want
his kindness again
I am thawing
                now

bulbs and seeds
distending holes
through earth and snow

        a confidence
fostered in a fallow darkness
cold and complete

reminding me how monotony
invites its own destruction

I delight
feeling the receding whiteness

            the retreat of features
            that stayed
            well past their season

        •

I think spring comes for all of us
there's no judgement in the thaw

of seeds scattered
long buried under frost
and lack of change

potency coiled
       compressed
implacable

When growth returns

the winter in me waits
like a child frozen
by their foster parents' stirring

as though the floor was littered with blades
waiting for the smallest twitch
      to score an opening

We aren't made for stillness
      the blood must do its work

•

You're a scar now
a depression
that I run my fingers over

grazing its lightness
        the mark of skin's memory

To skin, blood is a wildfire
no control over how much is lost
how much will dry
        crumble away
stay to form flesh

In the uncertainty of you
I felt like a fool
who couldn't look at a wound
                turned away
                denying the blood
                screaming

I wrote once that you felt like a scratch
        the newest part of me
        that I'm still afraid to look at

I don't know why –
all injuries
        new or old
feel the same to me now

no difference between

a room full of knives

and a tear in my skin
from which something might grow

•

The john would have known
if he stopped to listen –
        there are older
        darker memories
my skin was holding on to

He would have understood
if he cared to know me
past my body's impact
on his

He would know
that even
            accidents

can be transgressions
deserving repair
between equals

but
there's never been balance here

•

I love how characters
in epic movies from China

can bend themselves
around an attacker's thrusts

    like water around a charged rod
    light around a super massive object
    force woven into the response

denying the impact
    so that a fist or blade
    meets only air

frustration in their aggressor
building each time they
can't connect

I love the calm nature of it
like watching a burning wick
drown in hot wax

•

I'm not always allowed that kind of peace
but the thought brings me comfort
whenever
I need to retreat from my skin

•

It shouldn't surprise me
that when I upset someone
        they'll assert
        their world

repeat their understanding
                    often in anger

like they've worked so hard
to quiet the noise of me
rasp the colours, contours, and lines
that made me beautiful, overgrown
        and desired

and now must bleed the heat from me
for daring to grow through
                    a cold, familiar blanket
they'd worked so hard to perfect

forcing my stillness
squeezing against my
        every trembling

the gravity
of each clench
added to the last

        snow on a tired roof

tallying force
until I remain still

    amorphous
except for what

    they imagine
underneath

    •

It's strange how fear travels
flows back from wherever it lands

       as though something in my wounds might escape
       spray out
              injure the world

Should I be reviled
by the man who harmed me?

Like a fool who loosens a radiator cap too soon
       he's blaming the steam and hot fluid
       instead of his own hand

suspicious of what might return
       travelling along sightlines long buried

by a man certain
that harm only flows

downstream
       away from him

but secretly afraid
that blood
could crawl
against time
         return

step through the moments
that freed it

       to him

As though the memories
      behind the bleed
could impact him

the way
      the injury
destroyed me

   •

Connecting
should be easier

shouldn't come with this much resistance
and pain

Whether it was you
or the screaming man across from me

I feel like every time I try
someone is injured

my attempts
signalling the nature of harm

like skin stretching out
        beyond the tip of a knife
        yawning

hoarding the air around it
        seeking compensation
        for what the blade will take

After the dilating moments
the crackling split
        lightning through hot layers
above a pink bed
        reddening

I'm always pushing
hoping to avoid the inevitable

•

If feelings come in waves
then remembering is a shore
I've stuck
in the path of a swell
I can't see the bottom of
so I measure its
brutality
by the distance
between troughs
the balance of extremes
paid in destruction
a quickening mass
wedging and kneading
the rising bank
that presses back
dual compression
forcing salt waves
up
out
over
and through
what my island
had little time
to grow

•

I count
loops and tufts in the carpet under me
                    pausing at odd numbers

        silent
on the floor between the bed and dresser
                    knotted here

        by the john's focus
a glare that could siphon any refuge
                    water through clay

a demanding thirst
        I'd overlooked
        so old and regular
        it tangled

the two of us – ends of an unfinished pattern

That was, for me
        a narrowing, a
        tiny corridor crushed further

Was, for him
        a dark space between galaxies

Scowling at me, his
despairing clutch – his mind holding me
like a collapsing nebula
centripetal darkness

In light of that glare
      me
      seeing the pattern
      refusing

      turning away

   •

You asked about my brain. Wondered how I survive the constant checking.

I don't.

I explode every memory, kaleidoscoping patterns out of them. Every colour of a moment bursts into acute angles, perforating context, making a rabble out of simple interactions.

I know, it sounds beautiful – if you don't understand what clings to it, suckling like a lamprey . . .

On good days, I can ignore the fear.

But mostly, I'm a painful itch that grows into a gaping wound, because of hands that can't be convinced to stop.

•

It's been replaced. Now every night I wake to a dark room – different than the ones we get in Covenant House. No light can get in.

I walked to the hall, fearing something. You know that feeling when a cold shiver pushes you forward?

I turned a corner into a bathroom. I ran the water but heard a low moan. When I turned it off, the moaning stopped, but returned again with the water. I looked up and caught a face in the mirror.

The reflection was of a woman, with long, flat hair – and freckles. I tried to shake that face off, and it was blurred, briefly.

I opened my mouth to yell – help – but in the reflection the mouth only frowned as her face came back into view.

Finally, I gathered all the air I could and let out a scream – but her mouth only formed a circle, the moan returning.

Every night I try something different.

Whenever I scream it's always her.

•

Your fingers slide
over branches sealed in ice

The heat of your touch
teases water out
lubricating movement

and like a loose thread
your warmth unravels
a tranquil
        formless margin

You smile
seeing how quickly
the branch seeks to leave its cell

the water seeks to sever the cold
declaim its rigid
        former self

a relationship
        forged
in mutual alarm

the transient nature of winter
a smoothness the branch couldn't possess otherwise

•

I believe trees
to be so much stronger than us
        in the face of change

As winter approaches
a tree will slow its water
shed its leaves
and rest until the warmth returns

In spring, when you break its bark
        the sap flows, slowly
        and the tree recovers, remains

Unlike snow –

in spring, water flows unhinged
        escaping the sun
        its substance wild
        until there's nothing left

As a child, I would stomp through melting ice and snow
pretending I was a giant
destroying tiny buildings
constructed over millennia

I was the agent of time's impatience
feet falling hard against
what imaginary little men built

Now
I step on ice to hear it crack
a single
        neat sound – if I can

let the sun do the rest

        I'm not impatient for change anymore

because when spring comes for me
I still won't know my nature

        •

I don't care
for discrete things now

Simple edges
and neat boundaries
don't appeal to me the way they do
        to others

Perfection, like silence
is followed by madness

where your own body teases you
the sound of your own blood
        deafening

I want to be the discomfort
of bodies in too many sheets
where sweat wilts perfect corners
fermenting desire
        and binding

I want to spread the way water does through stone
seeping through places unseen
                a wet spot contradicting a barrier you thought perfect

I want to be the crack
in a building that makes
a landlord fear time
weather
and a long-term tenant

I want them

to fear us

      the way we once feared fever and cough

•

Brick walls
and a couch in the corner
where a photographer sat
        and smiled – me, weak

while his girlfriend watched from the bar

I sat on the balcony
        with close friends aware
that our return inside was anticipated
by eyes eager to see how we moved
        in youth

Whether we did it smoothly
strong and calculating
        as solid as their imagining

or if we moved like water
flexible and insistent

Every night, leaving
we passed
a jar holding biscotti
that no one bought

and a sign that read
                the bread that goes both ways

•

No one should
shape our beauty

     the canvas on which
     we splatter
     our collective sigh

after the struggle to find
safety
     is won

What's your age – in trauma years?

Trans moms
Charlene, Shawna Taylor, and Aman-duh
watched for us
where street
and bar lights couldn't

Behind green walls
darkened glass

we could dance
our freedoms
until our excesses
turned boring

as comforts
torn through judgement
hurt, and denial

grew lavish
immoderate
obscene
        traumatizing the world we'd escaped

A balance –

evening out the wrinkles
stretching oppression
in the opposite direction
            of a centre

too heavy to concede
a little brightness

    •

After sex
the photographer's hand on my chest
felt like it was reaching inside me
past every push my body could muster

Stillness my answer

And a hope that he could understand
the language of small movements
        that only the world
        outside our tormentors
        can see

The ceiling rolled through lights
that cars threw up
while his seiko echoed
off the bedroom corner
        a sympathetic language
        for the moment –

our pidgin for opposing worlds

On his bed, his sheets tickling
my foreskin already drying

I set out to remember every detail
about this moment

                except him

I used to hit leaves in the yard
with a hockey stick that had no blade
        forcing each one I hit
        against the wind, for a moment

It wasn't the futility of it that hooked me
it was the repetition

Inside the house, my dad would chew the ends of his fingers
until his nails were gone
while watching sports, saying nothing

I started to believe the furniture was eating him
and that more parts of him would disappear

if I didn't break him free of it

but whenever I tried to speak
fear would win

approaching me with the smoothness of a centipede at night
        crawling inside my mouth
        over my tonsils, down inside me
        resting inside my voice box

When I sat with my dad
it would grip tighter
swelling in my throat
pressing on my eyelids

until I gave up
and returned outside
to the certainty of leaves and wind

•

Intimacy now
feels like two buildings who watch the air
move freely between them
        hoping to join it

      mourning their hardness
      while the world plays around them

It's like baking a cake –
the guest is on their way
you're staring at the measuring cup
trying to will the flour into it
          realizing the flour was missing
          long before you thought to use it

Or visiting the bar at 17
spraying infectious laughter and insight all over
men who can't savour anything
beyond the way your jeans
      hang just above your tailbone

Or a crystal growing kit
stretching in a damp closet
of the house you can't return to

      an abandoned blossom
          unfolding in the darkness
unshared

It's every little thing made precious
because it never happened

•

I can't help but think that the couch
had a hunger for the joy my dad once brought me

our habits replacing
the brightness of his eyes around me

Sadness pulls a room like gravity
              a feeling the only reminder
              of what it was you missed

like the warmth of a hug
          fading

The men I chase now
are little more than cushions
air crowding sterile pockets when I stand
        their distending sighs
                 short, isolated
          potential

until I return

tricking them into thinking
I can be forever

    •

I would tell you more about my dad
except that I don't want to

He's mine

And joy is safest
inside the person who feels it

•

Dried blood
brown and greying
on a swab

is my favourite colour –

hues a mix of
rose petals and earth
      clouding

the memory of
red that flooded
      the syringe

richer than darkness
telling of the day's work

the burden
      of a long night
      bingeing

cradling toxic things

introduced
      but still needed
      in their time

    •

There's a richness
others can't accept –

with all the things inside you

that you'd still flow
thick with debris

stronger for what
it takes to remain wild
and fascinating

engaged in sex work
with men who'd reduce you to ash
                    the faded product of a spent force

But I like that –
being the dust of embers

barely visible
but for the impact of
            my decay

a suffusing collapse
fuelling blooms
that haven't yet
                found seeds

•

Today the YMCA / YSAP
worker asked   about patterns. She said
how   you were
                                      the beginning of

something
                                                        that
I've been   visiting
since:

                I figured if remembering   was like sandpaper
I   would have   already
reduced
everyone
to   the same   dulled
                low-resolution   shape and
                                            no one
                would be   unique

                enough
                for my
                skin

to notice.

You are
a hand mark   that stays
before   the blood

                    returns –

the impact of
your

dominance

                                        not yet ready
                                        to leave.

     •

I fear the unseen moments
that brought me here
    the loose cords
    of an unformed
    knot
        awaiting the pull

the way the body
gathers lethal elements for years
    a slow
determined
       saturation

or the hum of weariness
we wear like an old coat

where wet and cold
are preferred over
    a little nakedness

and we can't part with
what's killing us

    •

I want to ask johns
if I'm just a word
    to them

              prostie

unanchored
a continent floating
above a sea floor
with slopes and hills
that reach but can't touch
        connect
to this uniquely floating island –
      me

Am I a parcel
          a morsel
of neatly packed
meaning with
edges like tumblers
for their keyed fingers

         to enter
the way quays and docks
reach out into nothing
    on maps

and oceans
are named for the continents
that penetrate them

Do I exist to fill
a stranger's appetite

or are they vulnerable
enough to risk
conversation
        and a friendship?

Is there
something in the words
        street kid
        sex worker
        prostie
        Indian

that lets others breathe
knowing how far away
        we are

how unlikely
        we are
to puncture the sky
above their
        words?

But –

unlikely isn't impossible
and stiff
      inflexible barriers
shatter
      when pierced

    •

I find it strange
that a person can claim by

naming

that a speech act
carries authority

greater than the legends
                stories
        words
                        breath
                warmth
        heft
                and memory
of others

an embossing
on a land
already
        a home

        •

And yet here we are

A man I met on craigslist
told me he's Métis
with the conviction of a 13-year-old in love –
    a flood of warmth
    rushing out
    to hold what penetrated him –

unaware
that his admission
made us mirrors

parallel identities withheld
    until recognized

But that bed
was for expression
        not recognition

and I'm still trying
to limit what I am
    to moments

•

When you place your entire understanding in writing – a word, a story, a book – that writing is an easy mark to return to, should you lose the nature of who or what those words stood for.

You can set them aside somewhere and let them sit. They're kept words, static on the shelf – unchanging. You can be content that they'll never become something else over time.

Even statues weather and rust, but words don't.

You can return to them whenever you want, reach out and feel their images, their impact – ingest them again.

You are invigorated as you were the first time.

Almost –

there's something missing
when nothing changes

and stories
don't
grow

with their holder

What is the point
        of reliving

something

if it never changes?

•

Maybe it's not consistency
Canadians hold on to

but the lie –

that we can create anything
hoping it will stay exactly as it was
after the storm in which we created it
        has died

        that a man on a horse bronzed
        could be cherished now
        the way his soldiers
        exalted him then

        a man who designed an education
        can be spared our disgust
        because we've come to
        love schools now

I don't want that

I'd rather the purpose of our acts
spill out over the page they were designed on
        out over the next
        and over the next again
        until we don't recognize them

– though our descendants will

Anything we create
can't be forever

      shouldn't be the chain
that tethers a thrashed boat to the shore

It should be the water

    •

I showed these pages to the photographer
not out of love – don't worry –

but as a means of repaying him
in the currency he demanded

vulnerability

He liked the poem about bones
and how they bled

Fumbling, he suggested

periosteum

to use for the barrier
            through which I scored the marrow

thinking I needed the word
to describe it better

and that knowledge is neutral
        even when given

denying the pain and work
I needed to weave that picture –
            my picture

It felt like killing robins
because you believe all mornings
to be the same

•

I want our languages back

Where a word could have many meanings

depending on the speaker
the story they're in
or how they say it
or who is present

Each word filled with implications
like dirt –
        said to be one colour
        but holding a million
        particles

each wearing their own version of light

        •

Honestly
I think I'm letting the photographer
bother me longer
than I wanted him to

Using words like that
feels like trying to get to know someone
by the shape of their bones

too simple a rendering –
        like owning a land
        without ever seeing or feeling it

•

Time
it feels like
I've got the taste of

Watching sunlight sneak upward, climb my bedside table, and rest
on a blank notebook I haven't opened in months, I think –

Time stuck in my throat
fixed where I don't want it

while uncertainty invites another dusk in

growing in the space where my breath should be robbing me

Sun continued and cast shadows on a sock turned the colour
of bruises
torn off in anger after a winter's day of being alone once again

Thieving
sensations
others disregard

1, 3, 5, 7, 9 times
better-if-the-number-is-prime times –
every inhale
and exhale

deeply breathing, catch the air

is me

fearing the hollow
inside that

returns

chasing solace that refuses to stay forever

       Moonlight

    joins
    the fray
creating   art
    of
    clothing piles

clothing I
planned to wear

       discarded

   my brain
   skewering all hope

       to the floor
  again

  •

I don't know if hyperventilating in a room alone means I miss you
or if I'm just remembering us through the panic we shared

and I'm clawing at our trauma bonds
to bring back the feeling of you

with the same confusion
as a child
crying over empty boxes
trying to remember
a good Christmas

•

You can't claim to know someone
through memory alone –

there's never enough there

It's like a rock thrown across water

the force of it

                      fading

        as

   it rises

•

You have a yellow fleck in your eye. Have you noticed that?

You said that once. Lovers are easy to remember, and yet I only remember that about you. I could say there was a smell to you, or a feature for which you stood out to others. Maybe others gasped when you smiled, or your charm fumbled the hands of willful men.

But time is an acrid smoke, and so much has passed between us. All I can remember is your voice. Except that I can't remember your voice; just that it was your voice that put the yellow spot on a mirror around which this tired face grew.

Why don't eyes wrinkle?

Waking is difficult for me. Sharp memories rise quicker than my heart can modulate. I've traded my fear of false teeth for a fear of someone shattering my teeth. *Do you still have yours?*

We've fallen from a world of grass and flowerbeds into nails and hot irons. Gleefully they remake us into this: skin trying to cover injury and losing in the process.

I wish I could remember features that made you such a landmark, that bright smile in a post-bar glow, an exceptional moment nested in a murk of short interactions.

Maybe that was it. That you smiled at my imperfection without inhibition, and I'm fighting to figure out *why*.

If I could pluck a moment from time's needle I would sit and try.

Feel the reason for you, or the coolness of your cheek on mine. But all I remember is what you said:

You have a yellow fleck in your eye.

A flickering yellow shard sitting underneath water – nestled in white. The softest flesh I have, still easily preserved. And you noticed the imperfection.

Come back to me, please

so I can point out yours

•

One of the first words I learned –

animikiiwiyaab

When I questioned what that had to do with thunder
my friend smiled

I didn't notice how easily
we can apply others' meanings
to our own words

corrupting the relationship
subjugating half the picture

•

In English
you can name someone
without ever knowing them

The name
creates an outline

      a shape without texture
      a body untouched

that can stay unreal
and the person
is unknown
              unfelt
by you

I prefer names that demand a relationship

building with every exchange
a tangle of stalks
that flower together
growing fat with interpretation
      over time

   •

So many places
so many people
so many

lost their names
to English

•

Animikiig is just another form for thunder – with a missing meaning, until you see the clouds reach down splintering to push at the ground. They remain hidden behind the English version until you *see them* standing on bolts, riding the earth like it was a flood tide.

Thunder is only a warning until you're running away from it. The panic in one, two, and three one-thousands isn't real until you're trying to get through freshly turned fields, the mud grabbing your heels as scorched air murmurs danger.

I see now that I can't understand a word by knowing the definition alone
      I need the experience –

every word is just a sign post, pointing me to the moment I learned

      or *re*-learned

its significance

True meaning is a memory
scored deeply and beyond influence

   •

When Cynthia told us

that people walk around
with mirrors on their hands

pointed outward

I feared
that we are taken
consumed and held
by Canadians

with no significance to hold onto
outside of their vision

If theirs is the sight that matters
anyone can be you

step into your skin
when all other connections are gone

•

I think the introduction of an alphabet

       alphabetic literacy

to an oral culture

is like introducing hockey to a bunch of kids
       used to playing soccer

same amount of fun
and need for skill

but it costs more
       you don't share the equipment
       and not everyone can afford to play

   •

Wolves' dens
are rarely far from water

often facing it

and I realized
that is their ceremony

their chosen space honouring
the rhythm their bodies have found –

for the impressive amounts of water
they can drink
and must

      to ease the impact
      of that much meat

           uremic poisoning

– and I'm excited
for the ceremonies we'll create
to canonize our endurance

our ability
to dilute
so much

       (pain)

•

I think it's obvious that
    I can't shake

the photographer's influence

I loathe the way
he glances at these pages
and names the images

    dispassionately
leaching the colours

smug little bajaag

Still fucking him though

  •

There's something about men
and their fondness for ease

like me

I imagine they think
that money is simpler
than having to impress

      relieving themselves
      but no one else
      from the effort of courtship

Denying them their expectation
reveals the frenzied child
fingers clenched, eyes and mouth
           tapered

who was never far –
      there before the refusal
      and well before the idea

Because when they find I'm not

                              easy

they feel denied
robbed of something

as though I
were a continent that they could collect
because they didn't see anyone on it

and it's all so unfair
that it was claimed
      before they could arrive

•

Six hundred fucking years
and acquiescing to angry boys' demands
is still the rampant response

If this harm were purely physical
and we were all bleeding

would there be enough
to cover everything

      and start again?

•

Living in Canada
feels like fast words –
        utterances pushed out
by fear, alarm, and (pain)

a panic my mouth can barely
form around fast enough
to make sense of the tangle

like stepping on moss
covering submerged rocks
my loss of balance and certainty
                unending

Each year
each bruise
each removal
each death
each injury
each loss
each broken connection
each arrest
each unaddressed killing

each

        time we are named as if owned
        our Indigenous people

each confirmed belief that we are less
        and therefore earned

each harm

feels like pebbles in an avalanche
falling fast enough
to subdue and cut like teeth

but
none large enough
to take credit
for the deluge

•

This morning the photographer asked me to stop writing poetry as if you might read it. He said that you were the past that I didn't need to visit anymore.

I told him he was a shadow hovering over an already cold child.

The photographer demanded I appreciate all his effort. I told him I couldn't appreciate anything that tiny.

He left

Already I feel his words his impact being confined and evacuated. The way my body eliminates and expels any drug.

I liked him –

necessary, but not permanent

•

Every night it's a different face. Every night I try to scream, but the air around me resists – and it feels like exhaling through sand. My voice can't overtake her moan.

I try running, and the air holds me harder – like I'm trying to move through molten glass. Passing through the door, I collapse on a motel carpet, exhausted, but not from the effort – from age.

There's a shadowed figure there, sitting upright on the bed. I try to catch its features. I can only see a mouth – open, inhaling.

When I move closer, it opens wider. But there's no jaw to guide the mouth's movement. It's a free-form opening, reacting to my interest. When I move to one side, part of the mouth joins, and then the rest opens wider to accommodate.

I wait, quiet. I don't want the moan in the bathroom to greet me again.

Sensing my fear, the eyes open, taking a moment to find me.

I realize that its mouth is providing all sensation, and that it spoke with its eyes.

The bathroom evaporates.

Don't Speak, the shadow told me.

 Why not?

 It's not your place to.

What makes you say that?

Your anger makes you lack a legitimate voice.

Such a curious thing to say.

Of course not. Don't be curious.

•

I know someday
I should stop asking questions
        poking at the fog

and settle with what I know

but I fear that understanding
may never let me sit safely –

awareness always leads me to more
                scrutiny

and I'm not sure I can survive
the constant integration
of new experiences

I enjoy complacent, old
unbroken skin
        long free from incursion

I worry
there's not enough blood in me
to repair all the damage
that knowledge forces

        •

And I don't know how to feel –

where the memories of me sit

whether they live behind
the skin aroused
by my irregular panting

or entirely within language

I worry that my stories
will be lost to the world

a scattering –
        where no one holds all of me
no listener
no reader
no shadow on a bed
no lover at the end
        of an unsent letter's journey

no body large enough
        to display its earned scars

Or worse –
        that only words
will contain what's left

        •

My buddy's
tag is a cat
pointed ears
three rounded teeth
and a halo
The perfect image
a cat in sunshine
or of anyone
high or drunk in a park
with friends
His art is beautiful
and his friendship
is a late-afternoon glow
on a contented face
That tag brings a grin to me
every time I hear
someone lament its impact
on property value
because in me
his cat marks joy
knowing he's around
somewhere

•

I've gotten good
at describing the shape of my oppressor

without knowing how to counter their impact

It's like waking up
in the wrong geography
        adaptations circumscribed
by features you don't yet know –

being a horse without a herd
in a rocky desert
heat, scarcity, and boulders
making fun of its speed and endurance

or a donkey on a farm
                confined
dependent on people
to pare their hooves
the way freedom
and desert rock used to

or being forced to a new land
and told
that what you don't survive

others

just

might

•

I don't need to adapt

I need the landscape
        to change

    •

Every poem here
advanced past a break
        in my skin

opened by men
pressing for something
inside me

who were met with blood
rushing out
pulling tightly
reuniting broken fibres

Stopping the flow is impossible –
        because even the hardest things
        have cracks in them
and liquid always finds the opening

but like sea glass
solid things can't adapt
without losing their edges

This is why I'd rather
be the blood
than the knife

because both can fade
but only one can rebuild

·

I don't know where these words lead –
and there are more pages
        still empty

A person can't tell the future shape of a tree
by looking at sprouts

barely taller than ash and debris

But I know enough
to be certain
of the growth that follows

   •

I have so many now.

There's one where we were giants, playing with our size by falling over houses and trees, laughing.

There's another where I was racing the old ones in a game, and we stopped at lodges to collect keys that were dangling from the saplings.

Yet another, where an elder gave me white noodles, to take to the fire – as I approached it, I got so small that I could build my own house from the kindling.

And another – where an old nurse sat with me to tell me a story of her youth growing up with a white man who refused to teach her things. So, each night, she would free his horses. And the eagles would help her play jokes on him.

And another, and another, and another . . .

No longer just one

But I'll share those with you –

in time

•

Please
join me one day
tell a story or two

bring friends

•

When lava escapes
you can hear the earth sigh
watch a cloud of fury long in the making
paint the sky
Don't be fooled –
it's not the explosions you should fear
Be careful not to miss
the slow and certain crawl that follows –
when the earth moves like blood
fighting the air
breaking the ash-covered
walls of its last push
railing against its former self
The vibration, venting
sighs, and discharge
are the end of
a long dance
The eruption is our
anticipated recovery
the earth rising to swallow
its destroyer
The thrust and retreat
rise and erosion
twin processes
of a newly formed land
is a longer dance still

•

To ice

    water is lava

       and winter has ended

Ginanaakomigoom Nimishoomisinaanag

Learning is a lifelong process.

I chose to learn Severin Ojibwe while at the University of Toronto because it was the option that was closest to my people's language. I'm now eager to learn Plains Cree, and I know my experience will be much easier because of that choice.

I owe much to the former Anishinaabe Language teacher there, who was also my friend. Our time together has ended, but his impact remains. He fostered a curiosity and respect for the natural world, while encouraging me to find answers on my own – to do the work. I try to represent some of this approach in my creative writing.

If you are presented with the same choice – to learn with people of a closely related culture – do it. For the relationship, for increased understanding, for self-love, and most importantly because others long after you will experience the benefit of our collective effort.

Acknowledgements

Writing a second book is such a trip, and at times it felt like I had more questions about the process this time around. I'm incredibly thankful to my friends and family for your support through this.

Thank you to the staff at Brick Books for all the many things you do in support of our words.

I'm so very grateful, Ovila, for your cover design, and to Pat Ningewance for verifying the Ojibwe translations and orthography. Miigwech.

I'm indebted to Joshua Whitehead for your attention to detail and care in editing. You've done so much to help this work evolve, I'm incredibly thankful.

Finally, few people had as positive an impact on me as Susan Miner and the staff at Loft Street Outreach Services in Toronto. For all you've done, Gichi-miigwech!

TYLER PENNOCK is a two-spirit adoptee from a Cree and Métis family around the Lesser Slave Lake region of Alberta, and is a member of Sturgeon Lake Cree Nation. Their first book, *Bones* (Brick Books, 2020) was shortlisted for the Gerald Lampert Memorial Award and the Indigenous Voices Poetry Award. Tyler graduated from Guelph University's Creative Writing MFA program in 2013, and currently lives in Toronto.